BE STILL MY HEART

GENEVA
ENSIGN

BE STILL MY HEART

ISBN 978-0-9953437-3-3
Copyright © 2021 Geneva Ensign

Printed in Canada by:
UBR Services Printing & Copies
9618-B Bottom Wood Lake Road
Lake Country, British Columbia V4V 1S7
www.ubrservices.ca
2021

Dedicated to All
Who Search
For Something More…
And
Who Are Willing To
Dive to the
Depths
Of
Pain
And
Joy.

ACKNOWLEDGEMENTS

The heart on the cover photo has an interesting history and significance. My friend, Dr. Claudine Louis of the Samson First Nation, discovered this little heart buried in concrete at the site of the Powers Creek Falls, not far from my home in West Kelowna. Before the coming of the white man, this site was considered to be sacred, and it was used by the Elders of the Okanagan First Nations for healing ceremonies.

Later, the Gellatly family, new owners and farmers of the land, built a dam and cut a trough into the large rock outcropping to define where the water would spill over, thereby watering their crops.

It is currently a part of the Glen Canyon Regional Park, but its healing powers seem to remain, as its many visitors are soothed and enchanted by the rushing waters of the Falls.

I also want to acknowledge the Westbank Writers' Group, especially Donna Bird and Glenn Olien, for their continued encouragement and support during this time of Covid 19 isolation. Donna also donated her excellent editorial abilities. A huge debt of gratitude goes to Ursula Rymarchuk of UBR Services, Winfield, for cover design, layout and printing.

Thank you all.

"Ironic points of light flash out wherever the Just exchange their messages.
May I, composed of eros and of dust, show an affirming flame."
- W. H. Auden

A Few Words ...

As you browse through the pages of Be Still My Heart, a book of free-verse poetry, you will share moments in my transformational journey.

I have been on a life-long quest to answer the question, "Who Am I?" This question led me for many years to explore my Self at deeper and deeper levels, all the while learning to listen to the still small Voice within.

This transformational process has been called by many different names: Individuation, Self-Realization, Growing in Grace, The Red Road, The Path of the Heart. But whatever name it is given, the truth is that the deeper you enter into your heart of hearts, the core of your existence, there you find God.

Transformation happens in the midst of life; it is not separate from it. It is messy and life-changing, involving dreams, unnamed yearnings, deep feelings and synchronistic "happenings" which cannot be explained on a rational level. It is compelling, exciting, and awe-inspiring, sometimes joyful, but never boring. It compels each person to face the basic existential issues of life: freedom, responsibility, meaning and death.

Whenever I was in intense periods of Soul-searching, whether I was mopping the floor or walking along an ocean beach, free-verse poems, little gifts of awareness, seemed to write themselves. These were tucked away in a filing cabinet where they remained, unseen by others, for many years until my first book of poetry, Echoes From Another Shore, was published in 2019.

In simple words and everyday language, Be Still My Heart captures more of these moments along the path of my personal journey as I come to terms with the meaning of my life. Some poems were inspired by my clients during individual or group psychotherapy sessions. The poems are not in any chronological order, nor do they refer to any specific person. Hopefully the universal themes explored here will ring true for your life's journey as well.

"Be still and know that I am God."

POEMS

A BLUE BOWL

A blue bowl,
A gift
Symbolic
Of the bond
That unites
Us.

An act of faith,
This blue bowl
Bought in the mistiness
of
Transient clouds.

Not knowing, but feeling
Tentative bonds,
Believing yet
In old and
Ever-new beginnings.

Ancient
Merry-go-round,
Multi-leveled with
Pain
And
Joy.

Created from earth
And sky
And sea,
Forged in Fire,
Is this blue bowl
Unbreakable?

WHO CAN SAY?

Many people say
They know what life
Is all about.

Oh fools,
Do they?
Who can say,
You or me?
Who can correct
The intellect gone wrong,
Yet knowing not its error?

Not me,
Not you,
Then who?

A guru must surely know!

Thereafter, gurus of many ilk
I sought, but sadly
Their answers rang
Untrue
To my questing heart.

When, in quietude,
I sat alone,

And heard
A tiny voice that whispered …
The greatest truth
of all is
Love.

And Universal Love is all there is.

THE OLD STONE HOUSE

The old stone house
Is me
Strong, tall
Towering over the inert landscape
Sentinel to the night
Potential,
Possibilities unused,
Waiting behind
Layers of dust and
Outgrown clothing.

Waiting.

I'm tired of waiting and
Tired of
Wanting.

I can bring life to
This old house,
This shell.

I can bring back the warmth,
The fire
I can re-kindle the Spirit
Fulfill the possibilities,

The potentials.
And then,
I will live
In my house.
Alone, but
Complete.

Just me.

RIDING ON A DONKEY

Lord Jesus Christ, Son of David,
Foretold by the Prophets,
You came humbly,
Riding on a donkey.
Palms waving; people crying out
To you.

Did you enjoy your triumphal
Ride on that donkey,
Knowing
Who you are and were,
Knowing
That these same palm-waving
Followers would
Turn on you?

How did it feel,
This bicameral knowing,
Were you peaceful?
Were you dutiful?
Or
Was your heart breaking
For yourself
And
For this fickle crowd?

BEING DONE TO

When I lived in the North,
It was full of
Helpers, all
Zealously competing, even fighting,
For followers,
Patients
or
Clients.

Hoards converged on the Yukon
To "ize" ...

To
Organize
Civilize
Hypnotize
De-Alcholize
De-Nativeize
Christianize
Culturize
Womanize
Bureaucratize.

The list was endless.

A host of old-fashioned circuit-riding preachers
Descended
All at once upon the Yukon.

Strange that these new-age missionaries
Arrived at the peak
Of land claims negotiations,
The aroma of money pervading the atmosphere.

The question is:
Was I, too, one of them?

If I remember Biblical history,
Christ threw the money changers
Out of the Temple.

TO LIVE

To live is to love
> To love is to touch
>> To touch is to feel
>>> To feel is to know
>>>> The essence of life.

I've lived
> I've loved
>> I've touched
>>> I've felt
>>>> I know, now
>>>>> The essence of life.

ALONE

I am alone
All alone.
Alone amid the millions
Who exist alone.

A few touch me;
I love, I laugh,
I cry with them
While loving, laughing
And crying alone.

They love, they laugh,
They cry with me
While loving, laughing
And crying alone.

Alone, together
Alone apart

Alone, alone

All alone ...

COME TO THE CIRCLE

You were born to be somebody
Unique and special.
You have inner wisdom
That knows
What you need for your life's journey.

As a little child, things happened
That hurt you.
Unprotected,
You buried your feelings
So deeply that you didn't hurt
Anymore, pretending.

Grown up now,
You act the same,
Defensively,
Even though there's no need anymore
To protect
Your Self.

A Healing Circle
Is a place for new beginnings,

A place
To say hello to the real you,
To remember the past,
To re-feel and release the feelings,
And to realize
That you are not a victim
Any more.

You can choose new behaviours,
New ways of being.
You, only, are responsible for you.

Welcome to the Circle.

IN THE CIRCLE, WE ARE ONE

Deep in meditation one morning,
Images appeared
Before my unbelieving
Eyes.

Peering through the
Cathedral window,
I saw a Sundance,
Then peering through the
Sundance image,
I saw a cathedral.

Sacred spaces of worship,
Where we, each in our
Separate worlds,
In reverence sing
The Song Universal.

As I watched, both images,
Sundance and Cathedral,
Merged becoming
One huge heart,
Hovering o'er the clouds,
Elongating, transforming into
A tunnel,

Bidding me enter
To other worlds
Within.

In awe and wonder,
I followed along, only to find,
Deep within
My Inner Self, my Sanctuary,
Mine alone,
Yet
Not all alone, for my Sanctuary
Merged with others,
Forming a huge circle of
Shining light.

DISCOVERING

Learning is dis-cover-ing...
Knowing is a total "Aha!"
Mind, body, and soul,
In-liven-ing
Me!

ALIENATION

Alienation is
To be a stranger to my Self,
To be an
Alien.

Cut off from my roots,
My beliefs,
My knowing
About the world around,
I am a stranger in a strange land.

How then am I to walk?

STANDING IN A FIELD OF WHEAT

Standing in a vast
Field of wheat,
Divided by an ancient wooden fence,
I spied
Two eggs, very large,
On the other side.

As I gazed, they changed
Shape, Russian dolls,
That fit within each other,
Small on top; large on the bottom,
Like violin cases
Without lids.

Open to wind and rain
Without cover
Were these two male and female
Moulds they were,
Ancient moulds, and mouldy.

On this side of the
Ancient wooden fence, I discovered
The same forms, but
Much, much larger.

Shadows yet they were,
Unformed, but forming,
Not solidified.
No case confined them.

Not contained,
A flexible, flowing river
Of misty consciousness
Arose,
An infusion of new life
And energy
Into the ancient forms
In a field of wheat.

THIS STONE SPEAKS TO ME

This stone speaks to me
Tucked snugly up against my kitchen door
The morning after my brother's
Death
Tucked snugly, safely
A messenger he'd sent.

He said,
If he could,
He'd let me know his ETA at Heaven's door
Our parents on the other side,
Waiting eagerly.

Oh stone, round and rough
Ordinary and tough,
Magnificent and timeless,
From where did you come?

As messenger of safe arrival,
You now sit on my window sill,
Reminding me to continue
Our nightly conversations
Down here,
In my little house on the hill.

FREE SPIRIT

I have set a free Spirit
Loose in this world.

Where in the world
Do you think
She will fly?

What in the world
Do you think
She will be?

Fly, Free Spirit, Fly!

LET'S CANCEL YESTERDAY

Let's cancel
Yesterday;
Deliberately blot out
The hurts
And joys

That hang in the
Present
To curse
Our very efforts
To change.

Let's start with
Now.

FREEDOM TO BE ME

If I find
A tiny path,
One shining moment,
To my Self
And find,
In that moment,
Freedom
To be
Me,
Then
My journey has just begun.

I can forget, forgive, forego
The past.

Now
Is
All there is.

I will remain
Here,
Now,
And be
Me.

LIVING MAGICALLY

Living magically in the flow,
Two realities become one,
And I realize
Inadvertently I've danced through a rent
In the fabric of the universe
And entered a magical world,

Effortlessly traveling on an
Carpet of energy,
Hearing your voice in the breeze,
Warming my heart.

Realizing I too am an energy flow.

I am
I am
I am what I am.

Popeye was wise!

DON'T EVER

Don't ever leave
Me
Without saying goodbye
Because then
I would feel so alone,
Bereft
Of
You.

I AM

I am.
There is no beginning;
There is no end...
I am a circle,
Endless,
Perfect.

I am creation. I am life.
I am a breath of wind
Ruffling the leaves,
Whispering softly,
"I am."

I am a baby's cry
Soft at first,
Then insistent
Demanding milk,
Essence of life,
In order to be.
I am.

I am fire,
Burning,
Consuming -
Reducing all
To basic elements

In order to be
Re-created.
I am.

I am lightening
Flashing across the dark sky;
Energy, raw
Unleashed,
Recharging
Electrifying.
I am desire
Urgent,
Insistent
Surging to re-create.
I am.

I am the ocean,
Salty, endless swells
In the ebb and flow
Of the tide.
I am.

I am a tiny stream
Leaping over pebbles,
Rocks and boulders
Rushing to the sea.
I am clear sparking water,
Cold,

Moist,

Refreshing -
Life-sustaining.
I am.

I am a blade of grass,
Green in spring;
I am a sheaf of wheat,
Heavy with grain -
A robin's egg.
I am the sun,
Hot,
Radiating,
Energy.
I am.

I am.
There is no beginning;
There is no end ...
I am a circle,
Endless,
Perfect.
I am nothing;
I am all.
I am.

First published in
Echoes From Another Shore

INTER-COURSE

All of life
Is inter-course
Between layers of one's
Self...

Knowledge,
Skills,
Words
All left behind,
Shed like outer garments
On the doorstep
Of new worlds
Within.

MY MOTHER TAUGHT ME

My mother
Taught me
To make my bed,
Always,
To avoid catastrophes,
Like unexpected
Company
Dropping by and
The Pastor's Family
Would be judged,
Especially my mother
Who never felt good enough
To be
The Pastor's Wife.

She often fantasized
Donning wide-rimmed,
Very dark glasses,
Fleeing incognito
To some remote cabin
In the wilderness
Where, unknown to all,
No eyes could watch
Or judge
Or evaluate.

Sadly,
Even in her imagining
She could not
Shutter her own
Judgements,
Searching her Self
Again and again
For failures and
Limitations.

Yet,
She never failed
To make
Her bed.

My Need To Integrate

My need to
Integrate
All of life
Into
A rational,
Intellectual
Structure
Limits
My ability
To experience
What is.

If I allow
Myself
To experience only
What I
Can intellectually rationalize,
I circumscribe
My experiencing.

If I pre-judge what is,
I cut off
What could be.

Me.

ODE TO SPRING: THE DANCE OF LIFE

Ovaries,
Eggs and sperm,
Rhythmic dance of life
Sexual energy,
Desire translated into rhythm,
Pulsating beat
Energy stored
Urgent rhythm
Release.
Fertilized eggs
Microscopic ovals
Complete, perfect
Knowing,
Growing
In their perfection
Sheltered
Protected
Nurtured
In a warm
Enveloping
Expandable womb.

Growth,
Encompassed energy,
Pushing
Expanding
Dynamic
Slow, rhythmic
Pulsating
Sure, slow
Growth
Measured necessary moments
In the sheltered womb,
Protective boundaries
Burst open
To dance the dance
Of
Life.

No Defenses

With you,
I need no defenses,
I know I have said
That before
Yet now and again
I repeat it
In wonder and awe
Of your
Core.

DWARF YOU ARE

Dwarf,
You are.
Dwarf,
You will always be.

Spiritual dwarf
So tiny,
Tiny eyes,tiny ears.

Unused,
Members shrivel;
Atrophied limbs hang useless;
Sightless eyes are blind;
Ears are deaf
To life.

Your mouth is large;
Your body's bloated;
Your shoulders hunched,
Carrying your mind's enormous
Burdens.

Heavy step.
Heavy hand.
Hurting mouth.

Your Spirit's turned to gas,
Vulgar, noisy protests
Which you mistake
For sounds of life.

FIVE YEARS AGO TODAY

Five years ago today
I held your hand
And said goodbye
As
The tiny tube that gave you breath
Was oh so slowly
Removed
From the throat I dearly love.

Goodbye, Goodbye.

I didn't know then the depth
Of grief that I would know,
The yearnings that would visit
Me
Year upon year.

Yearnings for what?
For you, I know
And something more,
Something far beyond
The two of
Us.

ONE WAY

There is one way and only one
And yet its sides are two
I'm on the "in" side
On which side are you?

I've lived on the
Inside of a one-way communication line,
On the receiving end
Of God's commands,
Demands and restraints
As translated by
My mother
And by
My father
And later by
A would-be partner,
God's emissaries.

One-way communication
Enforced by loss of love,
Theirs or God's,
One and the same
Or so it seemed
At the time.

And soon, I was my own
Creator,
Creator of demands and expectations,
Endless, endless
Limitations,
Until …

SILENT SCREAMS

Silent screams
Locked deep within
By food,
By busy-ness
By no-thing-ness.

I'm lonely now, again
Lonely for connection
With
Some
Body.

Some
Body,
More than flesh,
A body, inspired by Spirit,
Alive.

Survival's not enough.
Plodding, plodding in oh so correct
And tiny steps.

Feet,
Take me out
Of here!

THE CREEPING CHILL

The cold
Is penetrating
My very skin
And bones;
The creeping chill
Is penetrating
My soul.

I long to be
Warmed.

REFLECTIONS ON A RELATIONSHIP

What I know, really know,
Comes from deep
Inside
Of me.

What you are,
Really are,
Affirms, facilitates and allows
Me
To explore a truth
Already here inside of me.

You help me most
When you are
Spontaneously and authentically
Your
Self.

Your very Being
In those moments
Helps me
Bring my truth
From there
To here.

IN PREPARATION FOR
SPREADING MY LOVE'S ASHES

In preparation for spreading my love's ashes
In faraway Nova Scotia,
I was drawn to
Peachland, our favourite place
To saunter along the water,
Contentment topped with
A cuppa and a tree hugger cookie
Blissfully shared at the
Bliss Bakery.

Proceeding on,
A tiny silver ring
I purchased from a
Kindly clerk at the Deja Vous boutique,
A man who remembered my Love
Fondly.

Leaving Deja Vous,
I heard my name as I'd oft
Heard before...
Thinking it was the kindly clerk,
I turned,
But he was busy with another;
He hadn't called my name.

There was no one there,
No-thing
But a warm, warm wind.
And then
A perfect heart, made of tar,
Cemented in the pavement
Showed itself to me,
As I opened the car door.

Ready now
As I made my way back to
Our
Little House on the Hill,
I returned
With a blessing.

Feeling able to be alone,
Knowing I'm not.

PULSE, PULSE, MY HEART

Pulse,
Pulse, my blood.

Pump,
Pump, my heart unseen,

Sending loving thoughts
Throughout
This world.

Sleeping giants
All are we,
Waiting, wanting to know
Who we are;
Waiting to awaken
From the dark, dark night.

Pump,
Pump, my heart,
Channel for the touch that
Warms dark, dark nights
And brings a ray of light, of love.

Pump,
Pump my heart.

OUT OF THE DEPTHS

Out of the depths
Of no-where
Comes a shout.

Hey there, hey there
Are you listening?
Can you hear my Voice?

So long I've been calling
You.

Come, take my hand
And side by side
We will walk
And talk.

You never walk
Alone.

PILGRIM, ONCE AGAIN

Pilgrim, once again
I am reminded that
I do indeed
Travel alone.

Alone.

And yet,
I have discovered
Moments of ecstasy,
Shining moments of joy,
Dewdrops,
That evaporate slowly
With life's routines
Leaving a residue,
A mineral deposit
Of solidified energy,
Strengthening
Me,
New fuel to continue
My journey.

Alone.

Inspired by Annie Dillard: Pilgrim at Tinker Creek

THE EYE OF GOD

The eye of God
Can only see
Through the
Eyes of
You and
Me.

Individuals,
Together,
Here we stand
To make this world
A different place,
We can.

THE CRICKET'S CALL

Little cricket, I hear
Your call
From where you sing
By my cottage wall.

Why do you sing at the end
Of the day?
What is it
You'd like to say?

****

Hear, hear, my friend!
Please hear me now.
Listen closely and
I'll tell you how.

The world must hear
Our cricket call
And the bees, the butterflies,
Sparrows and all.

Listen and heed
What we have to say.

We are dying in droves;
You are killing us all
With your pesticides, herbicides,
Germicides. What gaul!

What will you do
When no longer I call,
When the flowers don't bloom
And the sparrows can't sing?

You ask me why I'm a prophet of doom.
I speak for the bees and butterflies too
And even you humans,
Despite what you do.

It's a sad, criminal shame
That you want what you want
Despite all our warnings.
You must shoulder the blame.

You must gather together
All of you, all of us
To push back the clock,
And do what is needed
To save Mother Earth
And
All of us!

They Danced Out With His Casket

They danced out
With his casket,
Down the aisle
And out the door, singing
That familiar old hymn,
"We Shall See His Face."

Relatives in white,
Joined in the singing,
Following this unexpected hero,
Exuberance and sorrow
Mixed.

What will we do

When we see his face on
Billboards, banners and
Buildings dedicated to
This unexpected hero?

Did he ever dream
That he would
Change our world
In nine-plus minutes
Of time?

From here on,
What will we say;
What will we do
When we see the face?
Of this unexpected hero?

In honour of George Floyd
May 25, 2020

GIFTS FROM SPIRIT

Great Spirit,
You have consoled me
With your presence.
You have scattered hearts
Along my way
When I was lonely,
When I was sad.

Little gifts…
A heart-shaped leaf dropped
From a bird's beak,
A heart-shaped rock
Buried in the sand,
A rubber band carelessly dropped,
Turning Into a heart

Simple, simple tokens reminders
That I am not alone
Even when I think I am.
Instead
You are here;
You were here

Always here,
Re-Minding me.

A WIDOW'S INVENTORY

I am lonely here without you
Black Apache tears
Glisten translucent
In the sun.

I wrote this lament so long ago
When first
We were separated.

And now this year
Again,
I am lonely here without you,
So achingly, yearningly lonely.
Strange how life bends and breaks
Me to It's Will, not mine.

It's been…
633 days
15,192 hours
911,520 minutes
And
54,691,200 seconds
Since you left me.

This time
Forever.

I have come to the end of my running;
My house is clean
My freezer stocked
My lawn is mowed; my hedges trimmed
My weeds are pulled.
What next?

I'm not looking forward to winter
It will be dark, cold and lonely
Here
Without you.

HE SAT AND WAITED

He sat
And
Waited
Until
One day
He died,
Still waiting for
Some thing, some one
To
Rescue him
From
Himself.

Perhaps
His Soul
Did rescue
Him
From
His little ego self...

I do not know.

Anyway,
He died.

Is he now
Still waiting,
Confused and separated
From his Self,
His Soul?

I do not know.

DEAR GOD!

Dear God!
I am so lonely here
Without
Any
One,
Any
One
To laugh with me
To touch me
To be,
Just to be,
With me.

I am so lonely, dear, dear God.
Send me something, some one,
Please,
Some solace
To ease my aching
Loneliness.

****

My dear, dear, daughter,
I have often come to you in the night
While asleep you lie,
Unknowing, unaware.

I stroke your brow
And kiss your cheek
And say,
Be still, lonely heart, be still.
I am here
Always,
All
Ways.

CAUGHT AGAIN

A master game board
Our life
Is.

Caught
Again;
Do not pass
Go.

HOLY UNION

In love,
I walk with you,
My Self,
Complete
And
Whole.

Our holy union,
Marriage of God and woman,
Is blessed;
A chorus of heavenly angels
Sing
Allelulia.

Laugh, oh my Soul,
And
Be
De-lighted.

In joy,
I walk with you,
Oh, my Soul,
My God
My Self.

HELLO WINTER

Winter's coming

Winter's coming.

I've said goodbye to Fall, so sorry
To see her go;
Her golden leaves
Have fallen from the trees.

I've said goodbye to November,
With her chilly, chilly nights
And warming fires.

Regretfully, I recall
I've one month remaining;
Ere the calendar's turning.

Can I welcome Winter,
With her short and darkened days?
Can I gladly say hello to her?

I do not know what lies
Ahead for me
In Winter's snow.
I do not know.

SHE SITS THERE

She sits there
In an orange chair,
A queen enthroned,
Legs crossed gracefully,
Absorbing the April sun,
Wind blowing gently though her
Greying hair.

Mud and snow
Surface the frozen ground
Yet head and heart,
Sun and wind
Have melted their frozen north,
Gifting
Togetherness.

HURTS

Hurts inflicted
On myself
When searching
For The Truth

Are not the same

As hurts inflicted
On myself
As protection,
Prevention from
The Truth.

I Am Responsible

Whatever is done,
Whatever I do,
Must be a
Free decision,
My decision,

Made in full
Awareness
And
Responsibility,

Not in spite
Nor
In defiance,

Not with eyes averted
Nor in compliance.

I choose;
I act;
I experience.
I am responsible
For Me.

UNION

Our union was sanctified
In a church
In Calgary
By a Japanese minister.

We were not discussing
The problems of the inner city,
Which we were, but we
Presented ourselves, unknowingly
Before an altar,
Uplifted,
Surprised,
Moved
By a transcendent experience.

You said then that
If we only had time,
You would like
To sit
Side by side
In the cathedral for a while.

Instead,
We sat in your car;

Our next appointment cancelled, by
Coincidence or divine plan?
And talked of life
And love
Relationships and responsibilities.

I did not ask you to
My room, not then;
We drove instead
To the west,
Drove through the fog and mist.

You put your arm around me
And drew me close,
Asking quietly if it was okay.

Okay?
Of course.

Okay?
Hurray!

WITH YOU

With you
I can look at the flip side of every coin;
I can let myself become weak
Because of your strength.

I can let myself
Become judgemental
Because of your
Non-judgementalness.

I'll have to think some more on this
And explore what you have
Shown me
By your very be-ing.

With you I can explore
My weakness and my strength
Flowing from one state to another
With little resistance,
Not afraid
To be.

Not afraid
To be
Me.

WONDER WOMAN

Who are you,
Oh Wonder Woman
Emerging from a library book
So casually
Plucked from a shelf?

Are you my muse,
My inspiration,
Certainly a fellow
Light Bearer
Bravely holding aloft
That torch of
Inner Light.

I've lived so carefully,
Oh so careful, I've been,
Yet longing to burst
Forth
And dance,
Twirling in the light of
My inner knowing.

Lead on, Oh Wonder Woman.

YOUR HUGS ARE STRONGER NOW

Your hugs are stronger now,
You said,
They used to be so soft
And whispery.

Strong, tall and courageous
Now you stand,
Touched by the Great Spirit
And
Me.

ZEALOT AND PREACHER

Zealot and preacher
Would I be;
Hellfire and brimstone
Cast I on
Heads
Bowed in quiet defense
From my wrath.

Lost and stumbling souls,
Awake to my call.
I, Mother Nature,
Am calling
You!

Awake!
Awake!
Before it's too late

For you,
For me.

Please wake.

Wake!

WILL I KNOW?

Will I know
The pain of loving too much
Or not at all?
Will I know
The pain of losing too much
Or having it all?

OH OH OH

Oh, oh, oh.
I am so sad here without you.
Now that my busy-ness,
And my business,
Is over,
I have time for you,
My
Lover true.

I yearn for you.
And as I sweep dust from the
Corners of my house
And heart,
I find a note,
Written by you long ago.

I yearn for you
And your aroma, spicy and strong,
Drifts to me
On a warm summer breeze.

I yearn for you
And your reading light
Flickers on,
Then off.

I yearn for you
And Willie Nelson
Sings the September Song,
Our song.

It's one year
Since you left, yet,
You've been here all along,
Loving me
Laughing, riding on
Waves of synchronicity,

Magical moments enliven
My day and
Ease
This cloud of sadness.

Dark shadows fade
As remembrances of you
Bring
Joy
To my
Yearning heart.

DEATH OF A LOVE

Cold, so cold,
Creeping o'er the water,
And under,
Penetrating the depths
Stilling
Freezing
Solidifying
Amassing.
Seeming to conquer His spirit
Slumbering within.

Yet, look again,
An effervescent spirit
Grins and,
Released by the sun,
Dances
Sparkles
Arises
Returns
From whence he came.

Cyclical
Eternal
Mysterious
Is My Love.

WHY IS IT SO HARD?

Why is it
So
Hard to be.

Just to be.

Why is it so hard to
Set my Self free?

Let go; Let go.

Step back
Step kick.
Step back
Step kick.
Step back
Step kick.

Slow, Rhythmic Repetitions.

Learning slowly,
Learning rhythmically
Over and over.

Why is it so hard?

MOTHER'S FAVOURITE SONG

Mother's favourite song:
No
No
No
A thousand times No
I'd rather
Die
Than say
Yes.

My favourite song:
Yes
Yes
Yes
A thousand times Yes
I'd rather
Live
Than say
No.

LOVE, HONOUR AND CHERISH, BUT NOT OBEY

Love, honour and cherish,
That I promised him
But even then
Way back
Along our path
Together
I knew I could not,
Would not
Promise to obey.

Obey is a funny word
Crammed with meanings
Incomprehensible to me,
Implying: Master-slave;
Superior-inferior
Strength-weakness
Father-daughter.

Aware, yet not aware,
My Self,
Contained,
Slumbered in my youth,

Waiting.

My Gift From The Sea

My gift to you from the sea,
This tiny shell
Symbolic of
Another gift ungiven
Yet given
In Spirit.

That Spirit does not
Speak of surrender
Nor of rationality
Nor does it seek the reasons why,
But knows,
As it has always known,
The joy of communion
And the pain
Of reality.

INDIAN WOMAN

She walks through pain,
In queenly beauty,
Nourishing, protecting, guarding
The Spirit within.

Native,
Woman,
Guardian of Souls.

Beautiful
Eternal
Survivor.

TO LIVE EACH DAY OPEN

To live each day open,
Vulnerable,
Ready, but not demanding,
Is to face each moment
Fresh,
Anew.

To live each day open
To pain or hurt
Or disappointment,
Yet not be tense,
Nor fearful.

To live each day open
To love,
With the fresh innocence
Of a child,
Yet not to be naïve,
Is to be
Re-sponsive.

Response-able.

To Hear Your Voice

To hear your voice
Brings back the
Joy
Of our
Connection.

Beyond understanding,
It remains
Steadfast and solid.
Though worlds apart,
Still my heart
Knows.

I AND MY SURROUNDINGS ARE ONE

I and my surroundings
Are one.
I may live in a house,
Here on this tropical island
But the doors and windows are open,
Wide open,
And I am free
To merge with the outside.

Outside and inside mingle with
The ebb and flow of tides
Caused by the variance of the wind.
Like small fishes swimming in and out
Of submerged war tanks,
There are no barriers.
Windows and doors are gone.

My house, windows and doors open,
Lighted only by the sun or shadows,
Is a temporary place
To meditate, to organize or sleep.
I could easily do these outside.

The sea's temperature is only a slight difference
From the warm air
A secure, enveloping environment.

Clothes, a personal adornment,
Could be shed in a less inhabited place.

Oh, but, in Canada,
I guard against the onslaught,
Of the cold,
Layering my body with heavy woolen garments.
Hot, unnatural houses shield me from my environment,
Windows not only closed, but doubled;
Doors opened quickly and closed even faster,
Guarding against the icy blasts,
Using energy meant for communing
With my surroundings.

On Manus, this tropical isle,
Palm trees beckon with outstretched arms;
Gentle breezes skip over the water
The rhythmic wash of the water on sand
Emphasizes the slow, unhurried pace of life.

To rush, to be irritated, to be annoyed
Is out of character
With these surroundings.

This is my tranquility,
My pace,
My peace.

A DEER WALKS IN FEAR

A deer walks
In fear,
Tentatively poised for
Flight,
Her only protection.

A cat walks.
Connected
With herself
And with the ground.

A deer no longer,
I walk.

A PARTNERSHIP

An exclusive relationship
Of a
Man and a woman
Seems to me to have
A price attached,
An obligation of
Availability

Involving
What is needed to
Keep the partners,
And
Their two-way partnership,
Balanced:

Giving,
Getting,
Being.

Is that so much to ask?

ANGRY WORDS

Angry words
Tossed out
Carelessly
Bring
Pain and sorrow,
Forever marring
The canvas of our lives,
Forever black-marking
The invisible sheet
Of our love.

AND I AM AFRAID

Of irrational behavior
Of loss of love,
Or
My idea of what love can be,
Of being alone.

Yet,
Are we not
All

All Alone?

HAVE YOUR REVENGE

Have your revenge.
Go ahead,
Deny yourself
To me.
Feign sleep,
Pretend to miss
The cues
I sent your way.

You will say
You didn't realize
What the lighted lamp meant,
The silky gown …
You will say,
Why don't you ask
For what you want?

You will be innocent
All "in-no-sense"
In a sense,

Ah.

A ROAD IN THE WILDERNESS

To my brother,
Scenes of childhood
Come
One by one
Before my eyes.

Oh, my brother,
My playmate,
You were not ashamed,
Playing house
With me in the forest
Next to our small cabin
On what would be later called
The Ensign Road

Where, through sweat, muscle
And tenacity,
Our father cut down trees,
Pulled up stumps
And carved a road in the
Wilderness.

Oh, my brother,
Only we two are left
Who remember

Those days
And the courage of our parents,
Like Abraham of old,
To leave behind
All

To carve another kind
Of road
In the Wilderness,
An unknown road for us to follow,
Making it our own.

And now, you too, are gone;
And I am left
Remembering.

I ASKED FOR

I asked for a huge bucket of joy
And I received
Sadness and grief.

I asked for peace
And I received
Pain and turmoil.

I asked for trust
And I received
Betrayal and suspicion.

I asked for friendship
And I received
Indifference and resentment.

I asked for understanding
And then I Knew
That All I had received
Was as it should be,

Being trained to See
All
As
Love.

I Don't Need Your Affirmation

I don't need your affirmation;
I Know.

I don't need your affirmation
Of my "is-ness,"
My being.

I Am.

I Know.

I stand affirmed
By me.

By my Self.

TIMELESS SPIRIT

I am
That I am,
No past, no present, no future,
A timeless Spirit
In timelessness,
Body-less essence.

My body, a Temple
For Spirit,
Meeting place
Between
God and woman.

UNFREE FREEDOM

I am free
To explore
The recesses of
My mind,
To wander at leisure
In and out;
Bright sunlight
Shadowed recess,
Specific feelings,
Unnamed longings.

I am
Not free,
Yet, to give
Life to those longings
To allow the feelings
To be.

When one in mind
And body,
Whole,
Complete—then
I'll be free to see
What is
To be.

I Sit As At A Wake

I sit as at a
Wake

Head bowed, heart saddened

Watching the America
Of my childhood,
My beautiful America,
Go up in flames.

America,
Where truths are lies
And lies are truth,

Where hearts fill with hate
And reason is lost.

Some say that this chaos
Is a prelude
To new beginnings.
Could that be?
Is there now
A tiny stirring of hope?

I pray that it be so.

I WILL NOT SAY

I will not say
I love you
Out of any need
Or
Any desire to use
You
In some way.

The words,
I love you,
Will be saved
For a
State of wholeness,
Within,
Without.

WE STOOD ON THE MOUNTAIN

We stood on the mountain
In summer,
The four of us,
Partners all,
In glorious harmony joyously watching a kite soar,
Dipping and wheeling.

My friend saw
Herself, the kite,
Rising to new heights, free,
Except for everyday reality
Firmly attached.

And I
Saw the kite as a bird
Wanting to soar,
Taking off,
Flapping wildly, string attached
Pulled to earth each time.

Pulled by a string, tied securely
By my partner
Tugging often as a reminder
That he was there.

In October,
I looked again, same bird
Same string
But no other
Oh, not another,
Just Me!

I was holding my string
Pulling my Self back to earth
Lest I forget
My earth-boundedness,

Keeping my joy from happening,
Keeping my Self from soaring
To new heights.

IN RESPONSE TO YOU, LEONARD COHEN

True, true, true
Yet
False, false, false!

There may be no
Letters in the mailbox
Grapes on the vine
Seeds in the grapes
Chocolates in the wrapper
Leaves on the trees
Calls on the phone
Nor
A lover to hold me.

There is no-one, no-thing
Here
But
Me

And that
Should be enough.
Right?

MULTI-DIMENSIONAL MAN...

To the multi-dimensional
Man
Whose path
Inter-twined
With mine
In some mysterious
Way.

So short a time
And yet so long,
Time enough we had
To love,
To laugh,
To cry.

My dear Love,
I celebrate
You
On this
The first day
Of May.

MY FRIEND'S LOVER DIED TODAY

My friend's husband and lover
Died today, this morning
At nine o'clock.

He'd suffered endlessly
And she'd
Suffered bitterly,
Wondering if God is or isn't.

Wondering why God, whether he or she,
Would allow
Her Love's suffering,
Would allow cancer
To overcome
Such a good
And oh so kind a man.

And yet, and yet,
Look around.
One man's suffering, though one special man,
Is it greater far
Than the suffering of the masses?

If God sees the sparrow fall,
Does He or She see the millions
Who are being
Bombed, beaten, gassed, shot, raped, starved, drowned?

Oh God, where are you?

Have you come to us
Through the words and actions of Pope Francis,
Attempting to re-Mind us that your path is Love?

Can Love stop the assassin's bullet or the rapist's
brutality?
Can it roll back the darkness
And shine a light into our grimy souls?

LOVE IS A FEELING

Love is a feeling,
A force rising
Unbidden
From one's Inner Self
Encircling, swirling.

Love is Spirit,
A misty vapor
Beautiful and free
Answering no questions
Responding to no demands.

Love is.

TWO OLD PSYCHICS

Two old psychics
Together
Discuss
Interesting
Theories,
Material garnered from
Sources
Unknown
Or surmised.
Funny, how
Much we assume
And how little
We know
For sure.
Yet forever
We live
Unknowingly
Until
The heart
Is enlightened,
Informed and
Infused
By love and
By light
From the Soul.

THE FINITENESS OF TRYING

Ego draws attention
To its little self;

Spirit is self-less

Ego does;
Spirit allows.

Oh, the finiteness of trying.

ON LOVE

Love is not
A destructive force; it is
Constructive.

Love is
Providing security and warmth
And
Being sheltered within it.

Love is not
Selfish;
It is beyond its little self.

Love is
All encompassing
Without constriction.

Love is
Honest, open;
It is non-manipulative.

Learning to love is painful,
Giving up self-oriented, but lesser,
Goals is
Not easy.

Love is the expectation,
The encouragement
Of perfection without judgement
Of lesser attainment.

Love is unconditional.

Love is.

KNEEL AT THE ALTAR

Kneel at the altar
And surrender
Your ignorance and
Your arrogance and what you think
You know

For
What is not known
Lies far, far beyond that
Which is known.

Be still so you can
KNOW
What I, your Creator,
Would have you know.

Become a channel
For my Love
And I will fill you to overflowing.

Be still;
All is as it should be.

Be still, my Heart,
Wait patiently.

"What is left is simply, 'I Am'."

-Rollo May

www.ingramcontent.com/pod-product-compliance
Lightning Source LLC
Chambersburg PA
CBHW071945100426
42736CB00042B/2134